Lydia Shares Joy is inspired by the powerful biblical story of Lydia, which reveals the godly character a girl needs to develop as she shines for Jesus in this world. God's Word inspires, instructs, and encourages a girl to become the woman God created her to be.

In a world that recognizes earthly riches as success, we know that Lydia's story will remind young ladies to steward what God has given them, and in turn, be a blessing to others. Read more about Lydia in the Bible: Acts 16:14-16

Lydia Shares Joy

Written & Compiled
by Bianca Serfontein & Nicola Meyer
Illustrated
by Frances Tomaselli

For Danel van Lil,
for her generosity

Written & Compiled by Nicola Meyer & Bianca Serfontein
Illustrations by Frances Tomaselli
Printed in China.

www.thekristencollection.com

iDisciple

To:

_____

From:

_____

*L*ydia was so excited to choose something special for her sleepover. She was standing at the display counter in Blossom Bakery, clutching her purse that held her pocket money. Lydia was finding it a little difficult to choose the perfect cake or pastry. Mom just laughed as she patted Pip, their inquisitive French poodle.

Just then, a new tray of delectable goodies arrived, and Lydia lifted her nose to the air, instantly recognizing the smell. "Cupcakes! And not just any cupcakes – purple ones with yellow confetti on the top." Lydia and her mom both started to giggle. She finally knew what treat to get for her friends – her favorite color in the whole wide world was purple!

Lydia smiled as she remembered
the first playdate she had with her
friends, Rebecca and Hannah. All of
them happened to be at the library
for storytime with their moms. While
looking at the display of new books,
the three of them had reached for
the same book at the same time.
Lydia recognized both girls from
school, and she didn't waste any
time introducing herself. She loved
meeting new people and brightening
up their day.

Lydia's mom, Mrs. Peterson, had already
started talking to the other girls' moms.
Her favorite saying has always been
" 🐝 Be Grateful, 🐝 Be Generous." She
would say that each of us should be grateful
to Jesus and generous in sharing His love with
everyone. True to her motto, thirty minutes
later, all of them were back at the Peterson's
home having tea and playing dress-up!

Everything seemed to be ready for the
sleepover. Rebecca and Hannah would be
thrilled with the purple cupcakes. Lydia felt
determined to make this the best sleepover
ever! She had planned lots of fun games for
them to play, and they were looking forward
to working on their project. The girls had
volunteered for a project called,
"Helpful Hands." They had to come up
with an idea that would make a difference
in their community.

Lydia was so excited about this project because she knew in her heart that if each and every person did something, no matter how small, the world could truly be a better place.

Cupcakes ✓

Games ✓

Books ✓

She carefully added the finishing
touches to her sleepover preparations.
She loved to make her visitors feel
extra special.

"Oh dear, Pip! What have you done?"
Mom shrieked as she managed to
save the last two purple cupcakes.
Pip had eaten the sleepover
cupcakes. Devastated, Lydia cried,
"The sleepover is ruined! I wanted
everything to be perfect, and now
it's a mess."

Mom quickly came to the rescue, cuddling Lydia in her arms, "I know that this is terribly upsetting. When I am upset, I always remind myself to " 🐝 Be Grateful, 🐝 Be Generous." Realizing Lydia didn't seem convinced, Mom added, "Before disappointment clouds your joy, quickly find something to be grateful for and then be generous to forgive. Nobody is perfect... well, God is, so let's always remember to look to Him when we make a mistake or when we don't know what to do."

Lydia thought about this, "At least I have two cupcakes for my two friends; they will feel special." Mom smiled, "I am proud of you." She gestured to where Pip lay sulking on the porch. "Remember poor Pip; he could do with a bit of love."

Lydia joined Pip outside, this was one
of her favorite places to pray.

"Dear God, help me to 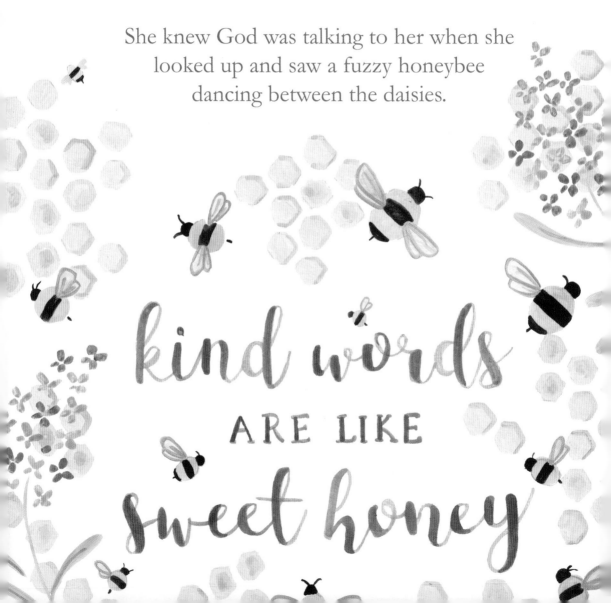 Be Grateful, Be Generous.
Please remove the sad feeling in my heart, Amen."

She ended her prayer and was reminded of one of her
favorite Bible verses, "Kind words are like sweet honey."

She knew God was talking to her when she
looked up and saw a fuzzy honeybee
dancing between the daisies.

kind words
ARE LIKE
sweet honey

Within minutes of her friends arriving, the house was filled with excited shrieks of joy. "Let's start with our project!" Lydia suggested.

"Should we pray about the project?"
she bravely added.
"How do you pray?" Rebecca cautiously asked.
Lydia tilted her head to the side, "Any which way
you would like. God loves me, and
I talk to Him all the time."
"Can you talk to God? Does He answer you?"
Rebecca questioned with surprise. She continued,
"I am afraid that I am not good enough for God
because I am not always very well-behaved."
Lydia smiled quietly to herself. She had been asking
God for a moment to share His generous love with
her friend. "He does answer you. It does not matter
what you have done; God loves us because He is
our Father. So, asking Him to help us with this
project is normal. Watch!"

"Dear Father, please help us to try our best and to work well together in this project, and most of all, to have fun!"

Rebecca looked astounded, "Is it as easy as that?" Lydia leaned forward, her eyes shining with love for her friend. "It is, Rebecca, would you like to have a relationship with God? He forgives us and washes us whiter than snow because He sent His son, Jesus, to die on the cross for us." Rebecca's eyes were wide with excitement, "I would! I know that He loves me. I am grateful to Him that He takes away all my mistakes, and I don't have to be perfect."

The girls prayed together. Hannah added with excitement, "God now shines in your heart, Rebecca! Together we can bring light to the world and make it a better place." The girls hugged each other, their hearts filled with joy.

"Snack time!" called Mom. They stopped at the top of the staircase, and Lydia called down, "Mom, please can we slide down?"

"Be careful, and hold tight!" she answered. Lydia kept a soft mattress at the top of the stairs. The girls cheered and hopped on excitedly, ready to experience the thrill of sliding down the stairs on a mattress.

Lydia let her friends slide down first. She followed behind them, giggling as they landed in a heap at the bottom.

Mrs. Peterson had set the tea table in hues of purple to match the beautiful cupcakes. Lydia smiled, "Go ahead, girls, guests get the best." Mom glanced lovingly at Lydia and whispered, " 🐝 Be Grateful, 🐝 Be Generous." Hannah and Rebecca loved the purple cupcakes. Hannah even suggested that they were too beautiful to eat.

Later that evening, they lay whispering in Lydia's room. Pip lay on the bed, sleeping soundly as the girls chatted.

"What made your heart sparkle today, Hannah?" Lydia asked. This was a game her parents had played with her since she was a little girl. "Mom says that when we remember the sparkle in our day, we remember to be grateful."

"I loved the cupcake treats!" smiled Hannah.

"And I love knowing that I have a Father who loves me," said Rebecca.

"And my heart sparkles when I spend time with my two best friends!" Lydia said, just before they all drifted peacefully to sleep.

The next morning, the girls woke early with big smiles. After breakfast, they joined Mrs. Peterson at her shop. She had started her dog grooming salon five years ago - Purple Paws Salon. Word quickly spread, and now she had the busiest salon in town. Lydia worked there on Saturdays to earn pocket money. She swept doggy hair, filled shampoo bottles, and sorted out all the accessories. It was hard work, but Lydia loved it! Her mom and dad often called her their busy little bee. She loved to be busy, and she loved to help others.

- purple paws salon -

On this particular Saturday, Mr. Jackson came to pick up Molly, his five-time-all-state champion poodle. Molly was a black poodle, who looked like dog royalty with her newly cleaned coat and diamond-studded collar. Mr. Jackson was telling Mom about the photoshoot Molly had been invited to. It was for a Doggy Calendar that would be printed and sold to raise funds for charity. "The proceeds from the sale of the calendars will be used to help raise funds for the church's outreach program to homeless people in the city. We hope to make a difference in their lives," he added.

Mr. Jackson's words "make a difference" caught Lydia's attention, and she suddenly remembered their own project, "Helpful Hands." Lydia often noticed the homeless people on the street and always prayed she could help them. This might be her opportunity.

Just then, Rebecca and Hannah's
moms arrived to collect them. Lydia was
left to contemplate how she could help the
outreach. She had pocket money saved, but that
wasn't enough. She had nothing of value to sell
either - and then she got it! Her heart started
beating faster. Lydia had an idea!

She wasted no time in texting Rebecca and
Hannah about her thoughts and plans for their
project. The replies quickly came back, high fives
and kisses. Her friends approved, and now Lydia
needed to let her parents in on her plan: to sew
and sell Purple Poodle Blankets! The profit from
the sales would then be donated to the homeless
shelter. This is how they could change the world
by making a difference in their community! One
Purple Poodle Blanket
at a time!

The three friends set about making plans and organizing all that needed to be done. Hannah's mom found them some beautiful, purple, fleecy fabric from a local shop. When the owner found out why the fabric was being bought, he offered a discounted price. Granny arrived later that day with some of her friends and their sewing machines. Rebecca's mom brought lots of sequins and iron-on paw patterns. The team was ready to get to work, and the Purple Poodle Blanket project was well on its way!

The house was filled with the happy sounds of clinking teacups, humming sewing machines, and chattering little girls hard at work. Pip loved all the attention and got lots of pats and cuddles from everyone. Lydia, Hannah, and Rebecca had drawn up a production line, and everyone set out to do their bit.

The grannies cut and sewed the little purple blankets.

Rebecca and Hannah's moms glued the sequins onto the fabric.

Mrs. Peterson ironed the silver poodle
paws onto the corners of the blanket.

Hannah wrapped
the blanket with
beautiful purple and
silver paper.

Rebecca neatly folded
each poodle blanket.

Lydia put the price tags on that said:
Please buy me to keep your poodle friend and someone
else warm! All proceeds will be donated to an outreach
program helping the homeless people in our city.

The team worked all day tirelessly, but Lydia worked the hardest. She made sure everything was well organized and that the production line was working smoothly. Lydia was like a busy bee darting between everyone. Eventually, the production line came to a happy halt. They were finished!

Lydia and her mom thanked
everyone for their help as they
left to go home. Mom turned
toward Lydia, "Your generosity
and hard work were a shining
light today. Well done, I am
so proud of you!"

The next morning, the three friends set up a little table outside Purple Paws Salon to sell their special Purple Poodle Blankets. The very first customer was Mr. Jackson, who thought it was a lovely blanket to put in Molly's carrier. The girls were thrilled when he bought an extra two, just in case. By lunchtime, the girls stared at their empty table - the blankets were SOLD OUT! After paying for their expenses, they had a $300 profit to give to their church outreach!

"I am so grateful!" Lydia sang as she
danced with Pip around her room.
"This was a terrific day!"
Mom came to tuck Lydia into bed;
it had been a busy few days.

"I thought you should also have one," Mom
said, and she handed Lydia a present. "Thank
you, thank you! You are the best mom in the
whole world." Lydia gratefully hugged her
own Purple Poodle Blanket.
She spread the blanket on her bed, and Pip
immediately snuggled on it. "But weren't
we sold out of all our blankets?" Lydia
gratefully questioned.

Mom hugged Lydia and tickled Pip's tummy.
"I asked Mr. Jackson to buy me one. You
were so busy helping others that you completely
forgot about our special Pip."

BE grateful BE generous

"I am so grateful God helped us with our project," Lydia said, still beaming from the day. Mom hugged Lydia, "I loved seeing your hard work being a blessing to others, my sweet, busy bee." Lydia reminded herself as she drifted off to sleep, "I am going to "🐝 Be Grateful, 🐝 Be Generous" for the rest of my life."

CHECK YOUR HEART

- Do you share with a grateful heart?

- Think about how you feel when you share with a friend.
  Another way to understand this is to ask yourself if your
  heart feels cheerful or happy?

- How do you show that you are grateful for what you have?

- Do you take care of your things?

- How do you feel when things aren't perfect?

BUILD YOUR HEART

- Before you start your day, think of three things you are grateful for. Keep a gratitude journal to remind you of the many things you can be grateful for.

- Read about Lydia from the Bible (Acts 16:14-16). She was a smart businesswoman who generously shared with those around her. Travelers and missionaries would regularly stay in her home. Her generosity, hospitality, and business skills provided her with many opportunities to share the gospel with others.

- Chat to an adult about ways you can help others.

- Decorate and fill a jar with reasons as to why you are grateful for a friend. Give it to them with a joyful heart.

- Practice doing your chores with a cheerful heart.

- Next time your friends come over, be generous and remember that guests get the best.

- Plan a sleepover or playdate; think about creative ways to make your friends feel special.

sleepover
to-do list:

• write a welcome note
• bake some cookies
• pick some flowers

HELP YOUR HEART

If you are having trouble learning how to share, you are not alone! Learning to share requires practice. Our shining light, Lydia, learned how to be grateful, be generous. We are grateful to God because every good and perfect gift comes from Him.

When our hearts are grateful, this helps us to share easily. You don't always have to share money or toys: you can share your smile, your time, your obedience, your forgiveness, or a kind word (Proverbs 16:24 and Acts 20:35). Freely you have received, so freely you can give (Matthew 10:8). God loves us unconditionally, which means that no matter what, God loves us, even when we make mistakes. Knowing this helps us to share His generous love with others. We do this when we treat other people with respect, kindness, and love. We also do this when we share the good news that Jesus loves us and died for us (Matthew 28:19 and John 3:16).

In our story, Lydia wanted everything to be perfect for her sleepover. She learned that only God is perfect. We can try our very best and then leave the rest up to Him (Proverbs 3:6).

The Bible reminds us to work excellently, with a cheerful heart, and to do everything as if for God and not for others' approval.

God wants His girls to be faithful with what He gives us. That means taking care of your possessions. He even says that he can trust us with bigger responsibilities when we are faithful with little things (Luke 16:10). He also encourages us to be generous, for it is more blessed to give than to receive (Acts 20:35).

CHANGE YOUR HEART

Dear Jesus,
There is so much I am thankful for…
Help me to never forget the importance of being
grateful so that I can be generous with a happy heart.
Fill my heart with love and kindness and help me
to be a shining light for You.
Help me to work hard with all my heart at
everything I do, because it is all for You.
Amen.